A Catholic Family Advent

PRAYERS *and* ACTIVITIES

SUSAN HINES-BRIGGER

Franciscan
MEDIA
Cincinnati, Ohio

Scripture passages have been taken from *New Revised Standard Version Bible,* copyright
©1989 by the Division of Christian Education of the National Council of the Churches
of Christ in the U.S.A., and used by permission. All rights reserved.

Cover and book design by Mark Sullivan

Photo credits:
iStockphoto (pgs. 6, 10, 12, 14, 16, 23, 27, 28, 30, 34, 38, 43, 44, 47, 48, 50, 55, 58, 61, 62)
PhotoXpress (pgs. 9, 24, 32, 37, 40, 52, 56, background images)
Veer (Cover image, pgs. 1, 3, 19)

LIBRARY OF CONGRESS CATALOGING-IN-PUBLICATION DATA
Hines-Brigger, Susan.
  A Catholic family Advent / Susan Hines-Brigger.
     p. cm.
  ISBN 978-1-61636-492-2 (alk. paper)
1. Advent—Prayers and devotions. 2. Families—Religious life. 3. Catholic Church—
Prayers and devotions. I. Title.
  BX2170.A4H56 2012
  242'.332—dc23

                        2012021194

ISBN 978-1-61636-492-2
Copyright ©2012, Susan Hines-Brigger. All rights reserved.

Published by Franciscan Media
28 W. Liberty St.
Cincinnati, OH 45202
www.FranciscanMedia.org

Printed in the United States of America.
Printed on acid-free paper.
12 13 14 15 16   5 4 3 2 1

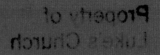

To my husband, Mark,
and my kids
— Maddie, Alex, Riley and Kacey —
for their love, constant support,
and inspiration.

Introduction

Advent is a funny season for families. The Catholic Church tells us, "When the Church celebrates the *liturgy of Advent* each year, she makes present this ancient expectancy of the Messiah, for by sharing in the long preparation for the Savior's first coming, the faithful renew their ardent desire for his second coming" (*Catechism of the Catholic Church,* 524, referencing Revelation 22:17). As such, we know that it is a season of preparation for Christmas, a time to ready our minds, hearts, and souls for the celebration of Jesus's birth at Christmas.

And yet too often, it seems as if Christmas itself arrives on the day after Thanksgiving—if not before. School pageants and choir performances, Christmas parties and gatherings, trips to nursing homes for caroling, decorations put up right after Thanksgiving and taken down December 26—all this would make us think that Advent is really just a synonym for the celebration of Christmas prior to its actual occurrence.

This little book will help put Advent in a better Catholic perspective. It does not deny the role of Christmas in preparing for the celebration of Jesus's birth (the actual Christmas season runs from December 25 to the Feast of the Epiphany), but it focuses on the beauty of Christian tradition in using the season of Advent as a time of quiet preparation for the Christmas feast. In fact, Advent was once a penitential season quite like Lent; the emphasis was

on repentance and conversion. Now we look on this time with hope and expectancy, much as the ancient people of Israel did in waiting for the birth of the Messiah, much as a pregnant woman waits for the birth of her child.

In *A Catholic Family Advent,* each day starts with a quote from one of the lectionary readings for the day. (If you would like to have all the lectionary readings for a particular day, go to the website of the USCCB. Their calendar provides links to all the readings.) This is followed by a brief reflection that talks about the Christmas symbol for that day. Next you will find a suggestion for family conversation about the symbol. This is followed by a prayer for your family to say aloud, and a suggested activity built around the symbol for the day.

The symbols and activities are arranged to give you time for a particular activity—perhaps an idea to make ornaments, Christmas cards, or wrapping paper early in the season so there is enough time to do this—but these times may not correspond to what works best for your family. In this light, you might want to read through the activities ahead of time and adapt them to your own schedule. The timing does not matter as much as the focus on preparing to celebrate the birth of Jesus in the best way possible for your family.

Because this is a book that can be used every year during Advent, it has in it the maximum number of days that can occur during the season of Advent. It will work this year and ten years from now.

With joy in our hearts, we await the coming of Jesus during this blessed time of Advent.

First Sunday in Advent

scripture

The days are surely coming, says the LORD, when I will fulfill the
promise I made to the house of Israel and the house of Judah

—*Jeremiah 33:14*

reflection

Nothing quite symbolizes the waiting that is a mark of
Advent like the Advent wreath. My kids revel in marking off
the weeks by lighting the four candles. As a society, we are
not really accustomed to waiting for things. Everything seems
to be fast—fast food, on-demand television, and instant
communication—thanks to smart phones and the Internet.
But Advent reminds us that, in time, good things will come.
Let's enjoy the wait.

talk together

What was the best thing you ever had to wait for?

prayer

Dear Lord, remind us to slow down and soak up the beauty of this season. Help us to not lose focus on the true meaning of these coming weeks.

activity

Does your family have an Advent wreath? If so, now is the time to get it out and set it up. If not, you can make one easily. Sometimes, parishes hold Advent wreath–making events. If your parish does not, you can purchase a wreath form made of wire or Styrofoam and fill it out with real or artificial evergreen branches. Don't have a form? Don't worry. Gather some evergreen branches and lay them in a circle around the candles. You will need three purple candles and one pink candle, but even that isn't mandatory. Find white candles and tie purple and pink ribbon around them. The important thing is to have something that helps your family mark the time through Advent.

First Monday in Advent

scripture

O house of Jacob,
come, let us walk
in the light of the LORD!

—*Isaiah 2:*

reflection

My daughter, Riley, hates the dark. In fact, she sleeps every night with a light on in her room and a flashlight under her pillow. When asked what she's afraid of, she says she doesn't know; the dark just makes her feel anxious. She has a point. There is something about the dark that can be scary. Maybe it is the unknown of what could be hidden in the dark. But, as Catholics, we take comfort in knowing that no matter what, we have the light of Christ to keep us safe and lead us where we need to go.

talk together

In what ways can you be a light for others?

prayer

Dear Lord, fill our lives with your light and lead us through the darkness.

activity

Pretend that there has been a power outage. Gather up a bunch of candles, turn off all the lights and spend the evening by candlelight. Light the first candle of the Advent wreath again. Play a board game, read, or just spend the time talking and reconnecting.

First Tuesday in Advent

scripture

A shoot shall come out from the stock of Jesse,
and a branch shall grow out of his roots.

—Isaiah 11:

reflection

Every year, my family goes to a local farm to get our Christmas
tree. It has been a tradition since I was a child, and it now
continues with my own children. I love watching year to year
as the trees in the fields grow. We all have roots, just like those
trees. And just like the shoots from the stock of Jesse, we will
certainly sprout other branches along the way. It is in this
growth that we discover where we are from, who we are, and
where we strive to go.

talk together

In what ways could your family grow stronger and develop deeper roots in your love for Jesus and others?

prayer

Dear Lord, in these days of waiting, help us to remember those from whom we come, who have laid the foundation for each of our stories. Guide us in your path as we continue to grow.

activity

Use this time before Christmas to make a few family ornaments for your tree this year (there are a number of books with ornament ideas from Catholic publishers, or go to http://www.ehow.com/list6887314catholic-christmas-crafts-children.html for ideas.) As you decorate your Christmas tree this year, talk about the significance of the ornaments or decorations you place on the tree. Add to your ornaments by buying a plain ornament and, together as a family, writing a prayer on it.

First Wednesday in Advent

scripture

Jesus called his disciples to him and said, "I have compassion for the crowd, because they have been with me now for three days and have nothing to eat; and I do not want to send them away hungry, for they might faint on the way."

—Matthew 15:32

reflection

My mom is an excellent cook. I love working side-by-side with her in the kitchen. It is the way we connect. Part of what I love about it is using treasured family recipes. We prepare and serve them in pots, pans, and serving dishes that have been passed down through the generations. For some reason those meals always taste better. Not just because my mom is such a good cook, but also because the food is fortified with years of love.

talk together

What is your favorite family recipe?

prayer

Dear Lord, nourish us not just with this food, but also with the love with which it was prepared.

activity

Prepare a special family recipe. Invite the kids into the kitchen to help you prepare it. Pull out the good dishes—you know, the ones you only use on special occasions—and use those for the meal. Talk about where those dishes came from and what memories they evoke. Begin to think about what type of meal you will have to celebrate Christmas this year, and what family traditions will be part of that meal.

First Thursday in Advent

scripture

Everyone then who hears these words of mine and acts on them will be like a wise man who built his house on rock.

—Matthew 7:24

reflection

My home is my refuge. I suspect it is like that for a lot of people. It is a place to shut out the world, relax, and reconnect with family. I think that is why I enjoy decorating it for the different seasons or special occasions. Surrounding myself with outward signs of those times reminds me to stop and rejoice. There is much in my life to be grateful for and celebrate. Decorating for those occasions provides me with a physical manifestation of that thankfulness.

talk together

Is there a certain decoration that embodies the Christmas season for you? What is it and why?

prayer

Lord, thank you for the blessing of a roof over our heads to keep our family safe and warm. Watch over those who are not so blessed with shelter.

activity

Form teams and divide up the rooms of your house. Over the course of the next few weeks, have each team decorate different rooms, but try to keep it a secret from the other teams. Use your imagination. During the week before Christmas, take a family tour to see each room's decorations. Have everyone say what they like best about each room.

First Friday in Advent

scripture

The LORD is my light and my salvation;
  whom shall I fear?
The LORD is the stronghold of my life;
  of whom shall I be afraid?

—Psalm 27:1

reflection

When my son, Alex, was very young, he spent a week in the hospital. Much of what happened in those days is a blur to me now, but I always remember the day a woman came into our room and handed me a blanket that had been handmade by a volunteer. Whenever I wrapped Alex in the blanket, he would immediately relax and fall asleep. No matter what age you are, there is something comforting and safe about wrapping yourself up in a warm blanket, especially as the weather turns colder.

talk together

What brings you comfort when you are afraid?

prayer

Dear Lord, thank you for the comfort and warmth of your love.

activity

Think about making a baby blanket for a local hospital or women's shelter. You can a try no-sew fleece blankets (directions are on the Internet) or, if you know how, crochet or knit a blanket. Another option is to find a way to bring some comfort to someone in need this Advent, perhaps a friend or neighbor who has lost a loved one, or a sick member of the parish. You can also visit a nursing home to brighten up the day of patients there.

First Saturday in Advent

scripture

When he entered the house, the blind men came to him; and Jesus said to them, "Do you believe that I am able to do this?" They said to him, "Yes, Lord."

—Matthew 9:28

reflection

Every year, I look forward to getting Christmas cards from family and friends, especially the ones that give me a quick rundown of what is going on in their family. Let's face it, we are all busy and, despite our best intentions, sometimes it is hard to keep up. But it is exactly those connections that provide a web of support in our lives. Family and friends are the embodiment of this season.

talk together

What has gone on in your life this past year that you would like to share with people?

prayer

Lord, protect our family and friends, who provide us love and support throughout the year.

activity

Rather than buy boxed cards from a store, create your own during Advent. Buy a box of blank cards—or make them out of construction paper or plain paper—and have the kids decorate them with crayons, stickers, or other embellishments. That way, each person on your Christmas card list gets a handmade and unique greeting from your family.

Second Sunday in Advent

scripture

I am confident of this, that the one who began a good work among you will bring it to completion by the day of Jesus Christ.

—Philippians 1:6

reflection

It is difficult to keep my children focused on the giving aspect of Christmas rather than the receiving part. It is hard to get them to focus on the needs of others when they are inundated with commercials and ads for the latest, greatest toys. During Advent, my husband, Mark, and I work hard to remind them that their truest blessings come not from receiving, but through giving and doing for others.

talk together

What are some good works your family could do during Advent to prepare for the celebration of Jesus's birth?

prayer

Lord, help us to be good stewards of the gifts which you have bestowed upon us. Lead us to those who may need our assistance.

activity

Who doesn't love a surprise? Place each family member's name in a bowl at dinnertime. Have each person choose one name—making sure it is not their own. That person is their secret buddy for Advent. During the next weeks, everyone should try to perform small, thoughtful tasks for their secret buddy. They might do one of his or her chores. Or, leave a note saying what they like most about their buddy—just remind them to disguise their handwriting. They might even make a small treat or gift. Encourage them to use their imaginations and not get caught!

Second Monday in Advent

scripture

The wilderness and the dry land shall be glad,
the desert shall rejoice and blossom;
like the crocus it shall blossom abundantly,
and rejoice with joy and singing.

—Isaiah 35:1–2

reflection

I love to garden. I love to grow different flowers and combinations to see what a beautiful landscape I can create. It never ceases to amaze me how two very different flowers can complement each other so well in my yard. Even in these winter months, I take comfort in those plants in my garden that withstand the season and provide me with beauty. In many ways, my garden reminds me a lot of the people in my life. We are all so very different, but complement each other well with our different personalities, strengths, and attributes.

talk together

How can you share your
talents with others
to create a beautiful
landscape?

prayer

Lord, help us to blossom
and share our beauty with
others through our talents, our
service, our selves.

activity

Want to brighten up a dreary winter day? Try forcing some
bulbs. You can do this with just about any of the spring
flowering bulbs, such as daffodils, tulips, or hyacinths. Many
stores sell kits with special vases, but I have found it just as
easy to place gravel in the bottom of a shallow pot, place the
bulb on top, and fill the container with water. For more ideas,
search the Internet or contact your local garden store.

Second Tuesday in Advent

scripture

O sing to the LORD a new song;

  sing to the LORD, all the earth.

Sing to the LORD, bless his name;

  tell of his salvation from day to day.

—Psalm 96:1–2

reflection

One of my favorite Christmas movies is *The Polar Express*. Every year my son, Alex, and I watch it together. In the movie, the main character receives a bell that he cannot hear. Only when he begins to believe in the magic of Christmas can he hear the bell ringing. These days, it is sometimes hard to believe in things. Try to focus on the goodness of the season. Listen to the joyous sounds and message, like the bell.

talk together

What do you love most about the Christmas season? What brings you joy?

prayer

Dear Lord, when we are faced with challenges, struggle and doubt, help us find joy.

activity

When I was younger, one of my favorite holiday projects was making jingle-bell bracelets. They are easy to make. Find something to string the small bells onto: yarn, ribbon, or elastic will do. Put on as many bells as you can while still having enough string to tie a knot to form the bracelet. If you would rather have a necklace, just make the string longer.

Second Wednesday in Advent

scripture

Those who wait for the Lord shall renew their strength,
   they shall mount up with wings like eagles,
they shall run and not be weary,
   they shall walk and not faint.

—Isaiah 40:31

reflection

This time of year is exhausting. Even when we try to scale back, there still seems to be a lot going on. Because I have a chronic illness, I have learned that if I do not take care of myself, I am no good to anyone else. As much as we all like to believe it, we are not superheroes. We need rest and time for ourselves. When we ignore those facts, we risk having it all come crashing down on us. In the end, if we do not take care of ourselves—especially at this time of year—we are setting ourselves up for a very unhappy holiday season.

talk together

What are some ways you can take care of yourself during Advent?

prayer

Dear Lord, remind us to be good stewards of our health—both mentally and physically. Remind us that we cannot care for others until we care for ourselves.

activity

Take a trip to a local park and take a walk or even just swing on the swings. The important thing is to just get outside and do something. Can't get outside? Enjoy some quiet time. Take a nap. Turn off the TV, radio, and phone, and just sit. Read a book or just sit and pray quietly.

Second Thursday in Advent

scripture

Truly I tell you, among those born of women no one has arisen greater than John the Baptist; yet the least in the kingdom of heaven is greater than he.

—Matthew 11:11

reflection

When I was young, one of my favorite parts of Christmas was setting up the crèche under our tree. In fact, my parents' figures of Mary, Joseph, and Jesus are all chipped because my sisters and I used to have them kiss each other and Jesus— you know, like a family does. A shepherd lost his hand when we had him hug Joseph. But my parents never scolded us for playing with the figures. In many ways, their "yes" brought the Christmas story to life for me.

talk together

Can you think of a time when you were unsure, but said "yes" to something and it led to a wonderful experience?

prayer

Dear Lord, let us be open to saying "yes" to new experiences in our lives, knowing you are always by our side.

activity

Does your family have a nativity scene? If it is not already out, unpack it and set it up together. If it is already out, take some time to decorate it. Make it worthy of Jesus's birth. Add some greenery or small potted plants—either real or fake. Make the stable comfortable for Jesus's arrival. You might even add some more animals or people from other playsets to help welcome Jesus.

Second Friday in Advent

scripture

But to what will I compare this generation? It is like children sitting in the market-places and calling to one another.

—Matthew 11:16

reflection

Around this time of year, children often lose sight of the true purpose of the Advent season—preparing to celebrate Jesus's birth. Unfortunately they are not alone—we adults also lose our way and get caught up in the frenzy of the pre-Christmas season. We worry about finding just the right gift, hanging just the right decorations, sending the right card. So many times I say I wish I could slow down, scale back, and reclaim the true meaning of Advent. The reality, though, is that I am the only one preventing that from happening.

talk together

What does Advent really mean to you?

prayer

Dear Lord, help us to keep our focus on the true meaning of this blessed season.

activity

When it comes to Christmas, parents tend to take a backseat to Santa Claus. Use that to your advantage. Write your children a note from Santa commenting on how their behavior has been or asking them to do something special for someone else. One year, my husband, Mark, and I put a few dollars in the letter with the explicit instructions—from Santa—that they were to spend the money on someone else. It was both interesting and heartwarming to see how the kids decided to use their funds.

Second Saturday in Advent

scripture

Happy are those who saw you
and were adorned with your love!
For we also shall surely live.

—Sirach 48:1

reflection

There are so many blessings we receive during the Christmas season (not just the gifts, kids!). We often have the chance to reconnect with family and friends either face-to-face or through Christmas cards. We also tend to reach out to others in our community, our neighborhood, and our parish to share events taking place at this time of year. Take the time to stop and rejoice in the wonderful gift that these people are in you life.

talk together

What was the best Christmas present you ever received?

prayer

Dear Lord, thank you for the blessings of friends and family, who bring such joy and happiness to our lives.

activity

Instead of buying wrapping paper for your presents, why not make your own? Take Kraft paper or butcher paper and let the kids decorate it with crayons, markers, paint, glitter, or stickers. You can also save the comic section from the Sunday newspaper, or paper bags from grocery and gift stores. Anything bright and colorful will do.

Third Sunday in Advent

scripture

Jesus said to them, "Whoever has two coats must share with anyone who has none; and whoever has food must do likewise."

—Luke 3:1

reflection

If there is one thing I have always tried to emphasize to my kids, it is how fortunate they are. Of course, because they are kids, they do not always get it. To them, it is just Mom saying one more thing. That is, until they came to pick me up from work one day and saw a homeless man sleeping on the steps of the church next door. They asked what he was doing, and I explained that he was probably homeless and had nowhere else to go. When I looked at them, I could tell they were having an "aha" moment. Suddenly, they had a face to put with my words.

Donation Box

talk together

If you had a lot of money, would you use it to help those less fortunate? How?

prayer

Lord, remind us to be thankful for all that we have, and to remember to help those who are not as fortunate.

activity

Many parishes and organizations have opportunities during Advent for families to help others in need. Take advantage of those opportunities. Go through your closets and donate nice, lightly used clothing, or collect your change during the month and make a donation to a charity on which you all decide.

Third Monday in Advent

scripture

> I see him, but not now;
>
>   I behold him, but not near—
>
> a star shall come out of Jacob,
>
>   and a scepter shall rise out of Israel;
>
> it shall crush the borderlands of Moab,
>
>   and the territory of all the Shethites.

—Numbers 24:17

reflection

Waiting for something—especially during Advent—can be really hard. The anticipation of what is to come can be overwhelming, and sometimes makes it hard to be on our best behavior. If there is a certain behavior I want one of my children to stop, I have found the best way to do it is to redirect his or her attention to something else. It is amazing how quickly they forget about what was capturing their attention before.

talk together

What was the hardest thing you ever had to wait for?

prayer

Lord, be with us as we await your birth. Help us find peace in our waiting.

activity

Cut up strips of brown and yellow paper. Each day have everyone in the family write down one good deed that they did that day. Lay the strips in your manger scene to prepare the crib for Jesus's birth.

Third Tuesday in Advent

scripture

For he delivers the needy when they call,

    the poor and those who have no helper.

He has pity on the weak and the needy,

    and saves the lives of the needy.

—Psalm 72:12–13

reflection

A part of my family's Advent tradition is to have everyone choose a name off the giving tree in the back of our parish church. The kids enjoy trying to find someone their age and maybe with similar interests. It is always eye-opening to me to see their reactions when they see those on the tree asking for basic things, rather than the latest, greatest toys. Sometimes, as parents, it is best to step back and let our kids come to those epiphanies on their own.

talk together

How does it make you feel when you are able to provide a gift for someone who may not have gotten one otherwise?

prayer

Lord, help us remain aware of those who are struggling during this time of year. Remind us how blessed we are.

activity

Have each person in your family select a name from your parish's giving tree and use their own money to buy the gift. Or, have everyone choose a charity and either use their own money or raise funds to buy something to help that organization. For instance, you could buy diapers for a local outreach to parents, or dog food or toys for the local animal shelter.

Third Wednesay in Advent

scripture

Jesus answered them, "Go and tell John what you have seen and heard: the blind receive their sight, the lame walk, the lepers are cleansed, the deaf hear, the dead are raised, the poor have good news brought to them."

—Luke 7:22

reflection

My kids love having sleepovers. Although I wish they would not stay up late giggling and talking in the dark, I remember that there is something magical about those late-night talks. I know how important my friends are to me, and I pray that my children will be fortunate enough to find lifelong friends who will love them for who they are and always be there to support them. Finding a true friend you can always count on and turn to truly is a blessing.

talk together

Who is your best friend? What do you like most about him or her?

prayer

O Lord, thank you for the friends with whom you have blessed us, and thank you for being our friend.

activity

Fill a small stocking for each of your friends with things you know they love. It doesn't have to be much—consider a candy bar, lip gloss, or a note telling your friend what you like about him or her.

Third Thursday in Advent

scripture

For the mountains may depart
   and the hills be removed,
but my steadfast love shall not depart from you,
   and my covenant of peace shall not be removed,
   says the LORD, who has compassion on you.

—Isaiah 54:10

reflection

The Christmas classic *It's a Wonderful Life* tells us, "every time a bell rings an angel gets his wings." Angels play a pretty big part in the Christmas story: They announce to Mary that she will be the mother of Jesus, they share the news of Mary's pregnancy with Joseph, and they announce Jesus's birth to the shepherds. Even in our own lives, we often speak of people who seem to be "angels" for us, helping us in a time of need, lifting our spirits, bringing good news, or showing up at just the right time. Perhaps that's why angels are so popular.

talk together

If an angel appeared to you in the same way Mary, Joseph, and the shepherds experienced, what would you do?

prayer

Dear Lord, open our minds and hearts to the good news that you send through your messengers.

activity

Grab some clothespins to make angel ornaments. For the wings, scrunch a sheet of tissue paper or a coffee filter and glue it to the back of the clothespin. Use a gold pipe cleaner for a halo and draw a face with a marker. You can hang them on your tree or give them to friends and family as a gift.

Third Friday in Advent

scripture

I have a testimony greater than John's. The works that the Father has given me to complete, the very works that I am doing, testify on my behalf that the Father has sent me.

—John 5:36

reflection

These days, people are much more on the go than during Mary and Elizabeth's time. We hop in our cars and head to the mall on a whim, run to the grocery, tote our kids to this practice and that friend's house. Recently I saw a slogan that said, "When things aren't adding up in life, try subtracting." There is some real wisdom to that. Slow down, take it easy.

talk together

What is one thing you can stop doing that would make your life less hectic?

prayer

Dear Lord, help us focus on what is really important and not just what we think is important.

activity

Stay put today. Aside from essential activities, such as going to work and school, try not to go anywhere. Sometime today, watch a Christmas movie or show together, make a meal at home, sit together for dinner, or play a game. Just be together—at least for one day—during this normally crazy season.

Third Saturday in Advent

scripture

Jacob called his sons, and said: "Gather around, that I may tell you what will happen to you in days to come.

Assemble and hear, O sons of Jacob;

   listen to Israel your father.

—Genesis 49:1–2

reflection

My dad has great stories. While growing up, I would listen to them for hours. Now my kids get the same kick out of hearing Grandpa talk about the old days. Those stories, however, carry with them insights and lessons that my children and I will carry with us throughout our lives. We can learn from those who have gone before us.

talk together

What is your favorite family story?

prayer

Dear Lord, keep watch over our family. Keep us safe and help us stay connected with one another.

activity

Gather up all the Christmas books in your house and sit together and read them aloud. Have each person pick a favorite book and read it, if possible, to the rest of the family. Ask each person what he or she likes best about the book.

Fourth Sunday in Advent

scripture

Your house and your kingdom shall be made sure forever before me; your throne shall be established forever.

—2 Samuel 7:16

reflection

A friend once told me that what he loved most about my parents was that their home was always open to friends and family. And that's true. I have tried to imitate that generosity in my own household. I am always happy to have my friends, family, and children's friends gathered around—a busy home is a happy home. Sometimes, though, we get too busy and forget to invite those we care about into our lives—and our homes.

talk together

If you could build a house anywhere, where would you build it? What would it look like?

prayer

Lord, watch over all those who enter this home. Thank you for blessing this house, and the friends and family who fill it.

activity

Host an open house with a few friends or neighbors. It may sound like a lot of work at this time of year, but it doesn't have to be. Ask everyone to bring something to eat or drink, or just order pizza. The important thing is to spend time together reconnecting. Talk, play games, or watch a movie.

Fourth Monday in Advent

scripture

The angel replied, "I am Gabriel. I stand in the presence of God, and I have been sent to speak to you and to bring you this good news."

—Luke 1:19

reflection

St. Augustine said that a person who sings "prays twice." If that's the case, then we do an awful lot of praying in our house. My son, Alex, is constantly singing. One time I asked him why he sings all the time and he simply said, "Because it makes me happy." That's a good enough reason for me.

talk together

What is your favorite Christmas song? What do you like about it?

prayer

O Lord, we sing your praises for all the good you have brought to our lives.

activity

Does anything say Christmas more than caroling? Gather family and friends and head out in your neighborhood to spread some Christmas cheer through song. When you are done, return home for some hot chocolate.

Fourth Tuesday in Advent

scripture

And now, your relative Elizabeth in her old age has also conceived a son; and this is the sixth month for her who was said to be barren. For nothing will be impossible with God.

—Luke 1:36

reflection

December brings the shortest days of the year to our country. The lack of natural light can make us feel dreary, tired, and less than joyful. We need light—our bodies crave it. Likewise, we need and crave the spiritual light we receive from Jesus's message. He is the Light of the World who helps us see through the darkness of our lives, and who shines in the love we show to others.

talk together

Is there a place in your family or community that can use some light? How can you bring Christ's light to that place?

prayer

Lord, bathe us in your light. Allow it to wash over us, filling us with renewed hope and energy to do your will.

activity

Even though the days may be filled with less light, the holiday season means that nights are often brightly lit with Christmas displays. Look around your home for sources of light. Bask in their glow. You might turn off all the lights and sit by the light of your Advent wreath, or take your family on a walk or drive around your neighborhood to look at the light displays.

Fourth Wednesday in Advent

scripture

O my dove, in the clefts of the rock,
in the covert of the cliff,
let me see your face,
let me hear your voice;
for your voice is sweet,
and your face is lovely.

—Song of Songs 2:14

reflection

My daughter Riley is an animal lover. After our dog Hobbes passed away, she carried around a ceramic Yorkshire—complete with Hobbes's old collar and leash—until we got a new puppy. Riley has great concern for all animals, including birds during the winter months. We are constantly filling our bird feeders, stringing popcorn, or throwing bread crumbs in our yard. It is no wonder, then, that her favorite saint is St. Francis, who was quite an animal lover himself.

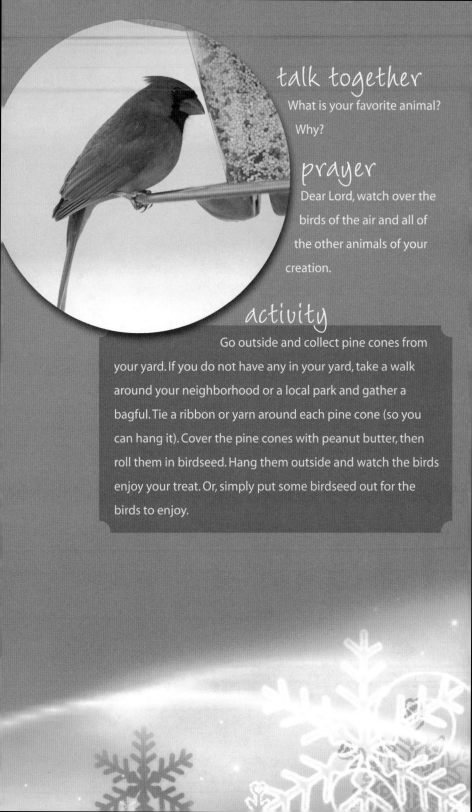

talk together

What is your favorite animal? Why?

prayer

Dear Lord, watch over the birds of the air and all of the other animals of your creation.

activity

Go outside and collect pine cones from your yard. If you do not have any in your yard, take a walk around your neighborhood or a local park and gather a bagful. Tie a ribbon or yarn around each pine cone (so you can hang it). Cover the pine cones with peanut butter, then roll them in birdseed. Hang them outside and watch the birds enjoy your treat. Or, simply put some birdseed out for the birds to enjoy.

Fourth Thursday in Advent

scripture

Mary remained with [Elizabeth] for about three months and then returned to her home.

—Luke 1:56

reflection

When my two sisters and I get together, we are always rehashing stories from our childhood—some good and some not so good. I always imagine Mary and Elizabeth doing the same thing, laughing, sharing pregnancy stories, confiding their hopes and fears, leaning on each other for support. The family connection is a strong one. And it is a blessing. As my oldest daughter, Maddie, said to her brother, Alex, once: "You have to love me. I'm your sister. You have no choice."

talk together

Recall a favorite family memory and talk about why it is so special to you

prayer

Lord, thank you for the love and support of our family. Be with those who are separated from the warmth and love of their families.

activity

Have a family photo shoot. Head to your closets or dress-up bin and put together a variety of outfits. Display the outfits in a fashion show, complete with someone taking photos. Judge the outfits based on made-up categories, such as "most elegant" or "silliest."

Fourth Friday in Advent

scripture

He has brought down the powerful from their thrones,
and lifted up the lowly;
he has filled the hungry with good things,
and sent the rich away empty.

—Luke 1:52–53

reflection

Baking is one of my favorite activities during Advent. Not only
does it result in something nice and tasty, but it also feeds my
soul to be surrounded by such wonderful smells and tastes.
For years, it has been a tradition with my mom, and now also
my children, to spend a day in the kitchen baking. And while
the plates of cookies we have at the end of the day are a nice
treat, the time spent together laughing
and sharing is even more rewarding.
Time moves fast; grab hold of
these precious moments
you can.

talk together

Is baking a part of your family's preparations for Christmas?
What are some of your other favorite traditions?

prayer

Thank you, God, for the opportunity to spend time together
as a family. Help us cherish those times.

activity

Bake some Christmas cookies from family recipes, or find
some new ones. Invite friends and family to bring their
favorite recipes and bake together. Have everyone tell the
story of the cookies that he or she is baking. Is it Grandma's
recipe? Is it a favorite from childhood? Let the kids decorate
the cookies. When you are done, put together plates of the
cookies and deliver them to neighbors, a nursing home,
or a hospital. Attach the recipes so recipients know the
ingredients (for allergy concerns) and can make some more
to share.

Christmas Eve

scripture

All this took place to fulfill what had been spoken by the Lord through the prophet:

"Look, the virgin shall conceive and bear a son,
and they shall name him Emmanuel,"
which means, "God is with us."

—Matthew 1:22–23

reflection

My favorite moment of every Advent is watching *A Charlie Brown Christmas* and getting to the scene where Linus recites the story of Jesus's birth from the Gospel of Luke. It puts the whole season into perspective. The signs and bumper stickers that read "Jesus is the reason for the season" are absolutely right. All that we celebrate during this Christmas season began with that birth so many years ago in a manger in Bethlehem.

talk together

What has been your favorite thing about this Advent season?

prayer

Dear Lord, thank you for the gift of your Son.

activity

Sometime today, gather together and read the story of Jesus's birth in Luke 2:1–20.

Christmas Day

scripture

All things came into being through him, and without him no
one thing came into being. What has come into being in him
was life, and the life was the light of all people.

—John 1:3

reflection

Birthdays in our family are a big deal. It is the day that
everyone celebrates the gift that you are to the world. I oft
try to let that person know what they mean to me, whethe
through a cake, a party, or a special dinner. Seeing all the
celebration that surrounds Jesus's birth
seems appropriate that we shou
likewise celebrate how spec
each of us is.

talk together

What gift would you have brought to Jesus if you had visited him in the manger?

prayer

Welcome, baby Jesus. Thank you for bringing light into our lives.

activity

As part of your Christmas meal, include a birthday cake for Jesus. Have everyone help decorate it. After dinner, light the candles and sing "Happy Birthday" to Jesus.

About the Author

SUSAN HINES-BRIGGER is managing editor of *St. Anthony Messenger,* for which she writes the "Catholic Mom Speaks" column. She lives in Cincinnati, Ohio, with her husband and four children. She writes "Too Tired to Blog."